ALL ABOUT TIME

Created by Gallimard Jeunesse and
André Verdet
Illustrated by Céline Bour-Chollet,
Daniel Moignot, and Donald Grant

A FIRST DISCOVERY BOOK

Cartwheel
·B·O·O·K·S·®

SCHOLASTIC INC.
New York   Toronto   London   Auckland   Sydney

Are you learning
how to tell time?

The cuckoo clock and the watch show
that it is one minute before twelve o'clock.
Count to 60 ...
then turn the page.

antique clock

alarm clock

wristwatch

One minute has passed.

cuckoo clock

Sixty seconds equal one minute.
Now it's twelve o'clock.

What time is it now?

The little hand shows the hours and
the big hand shows the minutes.
There are sixty minutes in one hour.

It is six o'clock in the
evening. It's time for
the park to
close.

The big hand
on a stopwatch
tells how many
seconds have passed.

This is a stopwatch.
It is used to time a race.

The small clock shows
the minutes.

An athlete who finishes a race in
the shortest time wins.

What can you do ...

in one second?

in fifteen minutes?

in one hour?

You can kick a ball.

You can read
a book.

You have time
for a long walk.

Long ago, people told time by watching the position of the sun, which seems to move across the sky all day long.

As the sun "moves," a shadow moves on an early clock called a sundial.

Do you see how the
shadow shows the time
on the sundial?

The day begins. You wake up.

When it is noon in Paris, France ...

When it is daytime on one side of the earth, it is nighttime on the other side.

it is five o'clock in the morning in Chicago.

Night comes. You go to sleep.

At midnight in Auckland,
New Zealand . . .

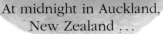
it is four-thirty in
the afternoon in Calcutta,
India.

By watching the sky,
you will see that the moon's shape seems to
change every night.

Try going outdoors to watch . . .

It takes about one month for
the moon to
go through its phases.

the moon going through its changes.

The seasons seem
to divide the
year ...

In the winter,
the day is short and the
night is long.

In the spring,
the day is as
long as
the night.

into four
parts.

In the fall,
as in the spring,
the day lasts as long
as the night.

In the summer,
the day is
longer than
the night.

There are
twelve months
in one year.

January

February

March

April

May

June

On the
Southern half
of the earth, the
seasons are
reversed.

July

October

August

November

September

December

Here's a story about three days in a row.

Yesterday,
I drew a picture of
my baby brother.

Today, I mailed the picture to my friend.

Tomorrow, my friend will receive the picture and be surprised.

Seven days make one week.
Four weeks make one month.
Twelve months make one year.
Each year you add another candle
to your birthday cake.

Three candles show that
you are three years old.

The years are going by.

Once
you were a baby
and could not walk.

Then
you could play and
read a book.

Now
you are probably big
enough to go to school!

Time is measured in seconds,
minutes, hours, days, weeks, months,
seasons, years, and generations.
Now you know a lot about time!

You can trace your family through the generations.
Find photos of your parents, grandparents,
and great-grandparents, and paste them
on the family tree!

Titles in the series of *First Discovery Books:*

Airplanes
  and Flying Machines
All About Time
Bears
Birds
Winner, 1993
Parents Magazine
"Best Books" Award
Boats
Winner, 1993
Parents Magazine
"Best Books" Award
The Camera
Winner, 1993
Parents Magazine
"Best Books" Award
Castles
Winner, 1993
Parents Magazine
"Best Books" Award

Cats
Colors
Dinosaurs
The Earth and Sky
The Egg
Winner, 1992
Parenting Magazine
Reading Magic Award
Flowers
Fruit
The Ladybug and
  Other Insects
Light
Musical Instruments
Pyramids
The Rain Forest
The River
Winner, 1993
Parents Magazine
"Best Books" Award

The Seashore
The Tree
Winner, 1992
Parenting Magazine
Reading Magic Award
Under the Ground
Vegetables in the
  Garden
Weather
Winner, 1992
Oppenheim Toy Portfolio
Gold Seal Award
Whales
Winner, 1993
Parents Magazine
"Best Books" Award

Library of Congress Cataloging-in-Publication Data available.

Originally published in France under the title *L'heure* by Editions Gallimard.

No part of this publication may be reproduced in whole or in part, or stored in a retrieval system, or transmitted in any form, or by any means, electronic, mechanical, photocopying, recording, or otherwise, without written permission of the publisher. For information regarding permission, write to Scholastic Inc., 555 Broadway, New York, NY 10012.

ISBN 0-590-42795-4

Copyright © 1992 by Editions Gallimard.
This edition English translation by Pamela Nelson.
All rights reserved. Published by Scholastic Inc., 555 Broadway, New York, NY 10012 by arrangement with Editions Gallimard•Jeunesse, 5 rue Sebastien-Bottin, F-75007, Paris, France.

CARTWHEEL BOOKS and the CARTWHEEL BOOKS logo are registered trademarks of Scholastic Inc.

12 11 10 9 8 7 6 5 4 3 2 1   5 6 7 8 9/9 0/0

Printed in Italy by Editoriale Libraria

First Scholastic printing, September 1995